This Book Belongs to
Elijah

Hey Elijah! Do you know who that is in the meadow?

It's a happy goat! Would you like to go to the meadow too?

Elijah, have you seen this fellow before?

It's a donkey who seems to love to walk around the lake, would you like to walk around the lake?

Elijah, what is happening here?
It's a sheep in the field!

Is that a cow over there?

Would you like to go to the countryside to see more cows, Elijah?

Wow, it looks like there is a pig enjoying the beautiful day!

Do you like pigs, Elijah?

Look who we have here. Isn't it a horse? The horse is running near the mountains. Would you like to run, Elijah?

Have you ever been to the countryside, Elijah?

Would you like to go to a farm to see a rooster?

Wow, Elijah, do you know what animal this is?

It is a rhino coming out of the water. Would you like to splash in the water like a rhino?

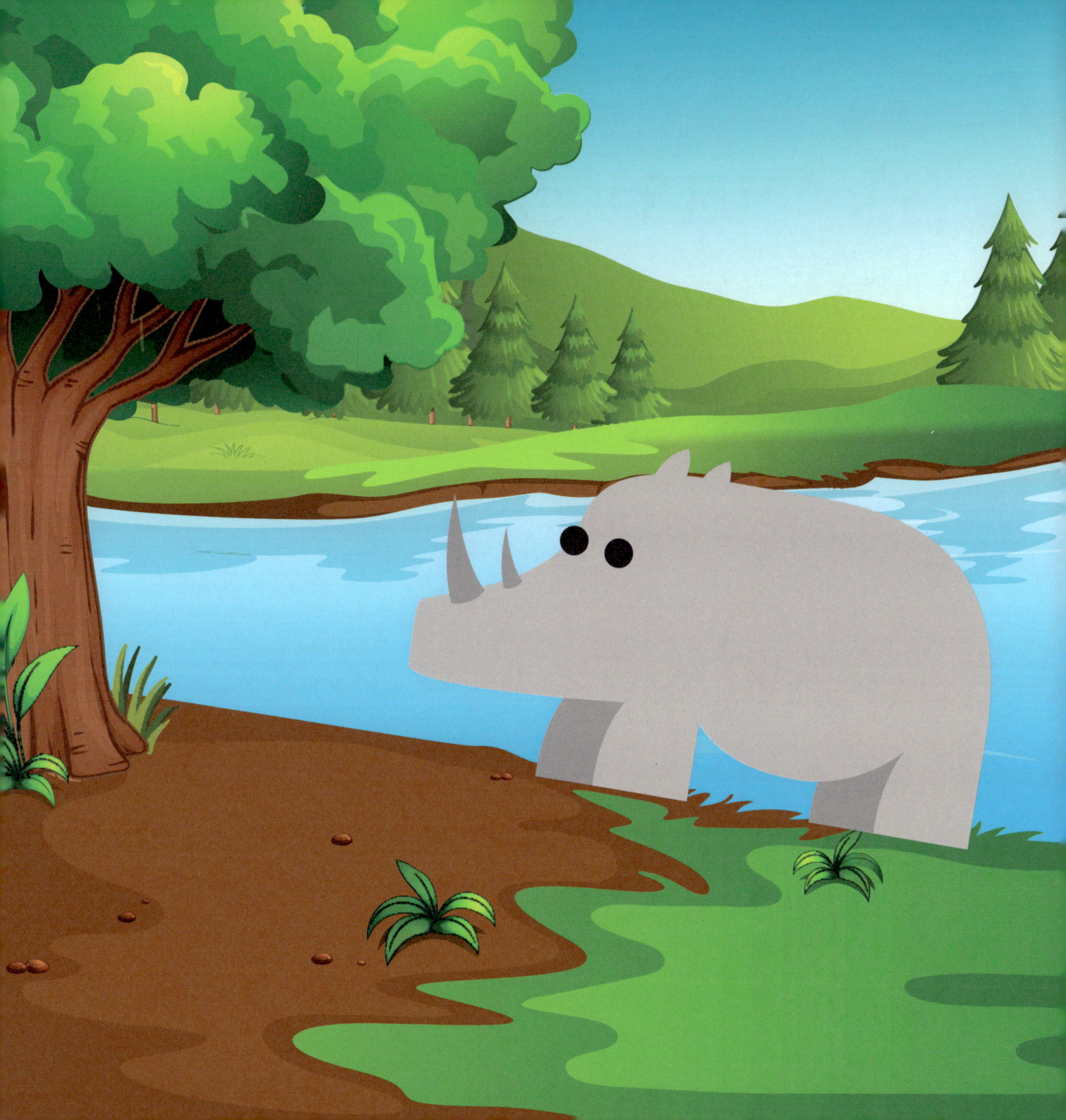

An owl is sitting in a tree so that it can easily see things further away.

Would you like to be like an owl, Elijah?

Look, it's a rabbit on the pier!
Elijah, do you like to hop around the lake like the rabbit does?

Here's a happy duck family, Elijah!

I hope you are as happy today as these ducks are!

See you again, Elijah!

Made in United States
Cleveland, OH
16 November 2024